Memory in Silhouette
Poems

Memory in Silhouette
Poems

T. L. Cooper

DEDICATION

I dedicate this book to
Loay Abu-Husein
Thank you for the memories we've shared!

ACKNOWLEDGMENTS

Eternal thanks to Loay Abu-Husein for providing the photo that became the cover as well as for his invaluable input and advice in creation of the cover. You will forever hold a special place in the memories held within my heart.

My undying gratitude and affection to friends, Kelly Gant Deaton, Lori Felmey, and Bryan Rader, who not only gave me their honest opinions about the cover and the poems within but offered encouragement and support whenever I stumbled. Each of you has helped me move forward in your own unique way, and your efforts are appreciated more than you know!

I owe a debt of appreciation to poet/songwriter, Tony Haynes, and authors, Pari Noskin Taichert, Joanne Pence, and Stacey Rourke for offering helpful suggestions regarding myriad aspects of Memory in Silhouette.

I could write an entire book filled with names of people who have offered me inspiration, support and encouragement throughout my writing career. Your contribution to my life has not gone unnoticed. Thank you for being part of my life.

Without those who read my work, writing would be pointless, so it is with heartfelt thanks I humbly present my work to you in hopes it enriches your life in some way!

Pointing Forward

Pointing forward
Even as memories
Deluge my present
Remind me of the past
Immerse me in your words
Drown me in regret
I hold my head up
Push those memories back
Remember they are over
Nothing can change them
They are what they are
For better or worse
Those memories remind me
Ignoring them belittles their lessons
Makes me forget my growth
Encourages me to repeat the mistakes
Embracing those memories
Frightens me
Reminds me what I abandoned
Teases me with what worked
Taunts me with "what ifs" I can't change
So I square my shoulders
Give my memories recognition
They helped me become me
They remind me to keep
Pointing forward
Even when
Pointing forward
Feels like taking a step back
Into memories that matter
Into memories that hurt

Into memories that uplifted
Into memories that changed me
Whether I like it or not
My memories are instrumental
In me
Pointing forward

Nostalgia

Nostalgia opens the vein of melancholy
Memories pour over my skin
Flooding me with moments lost to time
Drowning me in yesterday
Giving me pause as I reach for today
Reminding me what I abandoned
Aching with the regret of pain inflicted
I watch from somewhere outside myself
Wishing for the lifeline I severed
Opening the scars of memory's wounds
The blistering of our passion's burn
The sting of the laughter we shared turning to tears
The frostbite of our love freezing between us
The bruise left in the place where your arms embraced me
The cut of the emptiness of life without you
Grasping for hope within each scar's opening
Wishing for a fresh skin, an un-marred heart, healing
Perhaps I should drown myself in the nostalgia
Allow the vein of melancholy to bleed me free from you
Nostalgia opens the vein of melancholy

Suitcase of Memories

Yesterday I opened
A suitcase of memories
We created
We hid away
To enjoy another day
Forgot them
Didn't cherish them
Didn't appreciate them
Decided they weren't good enough
I stared into
A suitcase of our memories
I ran my fingers through them
Looking for one to close the gap
Tears filled my eyes
As I realized
All those memories we should have
Cherished
Appreciated
Valued
Had turned to sand
Leaving us with no
Foundation to build upon

Touch of Memory

The touch of your memory
Skates across my skin
Sets my nerve endings on fire
Freezes my cells in place
Lingers in the air around me
The touch of your memory
Shows up unexpected, uninvited, unannounced
Caresses my emotions
Toys with my thoughts
Plays with my fantasies
Fills my emptiness with hope
Invades my life
Breaks my heart into pieces
Brings you from then to now
The touch of your memory
Glues me to you
Holds you in me
Makes me long for more
Teases me with possibility
Terrifies me
Empowers me
The touch of your memory
Lives in my cells
Tingles along my skin
Revives long hidden emotions
Makes me wonder what to do with
The touch of your memory

Memory of Intimacy

It's one twenty-nine in the morning
I lay awake
Having just written you a letter I'll never send
Crying tears you'll never see
Regretting words I'll never say
Wishing moments that'll never be
Longing for courage I'll never have
The quiet in the room
Feels heavy with memory
Wet with desire as I breathe it in
Breaking it feels like sacrilege so I whisper your name
A cry escaping from my lips against my will
The wind outside reaches across the distance to you
And I wonder if you feel me touch your soul
With my thoughts, my regrets, my heartache
The miles between us have grown into more than distance
They symbolize the words we don't say
They represent the emotions we hide
They give excuse to the separate lives we lead
They render us powerless to explore what could be
They conceal the fantasy we share
Technology makes it seem we're in the same room
We reach for an intimacy that is fleeting
We pretend the distance can melt away in a moment
We realize it's not quite enough
And we long
For something more real
The memory of touch
Isn't the same as sharing a caress
The memory of taste
Isn't the same as the urgency of a kiss

The memory of intimacy
Isn't the same as two bodies connecting
The fantasy of us
Becomes a longing that can't be fulfilled
It's now one forty-three in the morning
And I still can't quit wondering
If we'll ever again share the intimacy that should be ours
Instead of clinging to this
Memory of intimacy

Crush

I awaken at three in the morning
I'm sure I hear your voice
Calling out to me
Yet you're not there
The emptiness in the room
Weighs on top of me
Crushing the air from my lungs
I welcome the pain
Your absence is heavier than your presence ever was
I reach into the void
Where you should be
The abyss in my life
That can only be filled by you
I wonder if you're awake as well
And if you are
Is it because you hear my voice
Calling out to you
Even though I'm not there
Does the emptiness in your room
Weigh on top of you
Crushing the air from your lungs
Do you welcome the pain
Is my absence heavier than my presence ever was
Do you reach into the emptiness
Where I should be
Is there a void I left in your life
That can only be filled by me
Will we ever break down
And admit this is more than an attraction
Or are we too afraid of the connection
We can't seem to escape

This pretense we live that keeps us apart
This past we can't escape
This absence we share that crushes us both

Taunted

Haunted by your kiss
Possessed by your caress
Encapsulated by your embrace
Taunted by memories
Longing for another chance
To rekindle the fire I extinguished
To remind you what you once saw in me
To remember what I never forgot
All those days
All those nights
All those moments
We shared with abandon
We laughed
We touched
We dreamed
We consoled
We planned
How is it that all that's left
Are the memories that taunt me
Your inviting smile
Your loving eyes
You passion
Your touch
Your sense of humor
Your love
I ponder possibilities
I long for you to reach out
I remain
Forever
Taunted

Me Either

Remember the day
We ran barefoot
Through the wet bluegrass of Kentucky
Holding hands
Me either

Remember the day
We rolled off our picnic blanket
Onto the crumbly, dry grass
Holding one another tight
Me either

Remember the day
We laughed for hours
Pulling blades of grass from the earth
Sitting side by side, bent legs touching
Me either

Remember the day
We searched for answers in one another's eyes
Sitting cross-legged on the bright green grass
Our feet and knees touching
Me either

Remember the day
We talked for hours
The sun shining off the grass, tinting it blue
Our words, our energy intertwined
Me either

Remember the day

We shared our dreams
Crushing the grass beneath us
As I sat on your lap, my arms around your neck
Me either

Remember the day
We exposed our deepest, darkest secrets
As the grass waved in the wind, exposing the blue tint
Your fingers gently stroking my tearstained cheek
Me either

Remember the day
We first realized the depths of our emotions
The green grass on the hill reflected in the pond
Our lips finding passion as they touched
Me either

Remember the day
We walked our separate ways
Rain pelting on the grass
Our bodies pulling us back for one more embrace
Me either

Remember the day
We no longer were a we
Snow hiding the green grass
Our lives too far apart to feel the touch we cherished
Me either

Remember the day
We were entwined in perfection
The bluegrass of Kentucky under us
Wondering if we were dreaming
Me either

Remember the day
We existed as a we
Taking for granted the bluegrass between our toes
Ever wonder if it really happened
Me either

Magic, Black or White

You stared into my eyes
On that bright, sunny afternoon
Bewitched by my innocent smile
Charmed by my sweet words
Enchanted by my attentive nod
You stepped back as the clouds covered the sun
A shadow falling over our intimacy
Leaning forward your lips touched mine
Lightly almost imperceptibly
Your finger trailed gently over the goose bumps on my arm
As the hot wind suddenly chilled
Our gaze trapped one another in the moment
Entranced we couldn't step away
Sudden, heavy rain pelted us
And still we stood
Slowly your arms encircled my waist
You pulled me tight to you
A kiss most urgent expressed your hunger
Drenched, we remained as the sun returned
Beating heat upon our chilled bodies
You pulled me closer
Held me tighter
Until our shadows became one
Hearts pounding in perfect rhythm
Our bodies knowing the answer
We dared not question
Life pounding through us
Love pouring out of us
Passion steaming from us
You tilted my chin up
Looked into my eyes and whispered

"My sweet woman, you are magic itself
Black or white
If you're giving it, I'll take it."
I blinked back a tear and whispered
"Honey, magic is only magic
Black or white
When two people both freely partake."
Your kiss captured my words
And magic
Black or white, perhaps both,
Filled us, flowed from us, flamed around us

Moonlight

I stare into
The moon's face
Through the window
From the safety of my room
From the security of distance
Does the moon remember
Do you remember
Midnight walks we shared
Sly touches of skin
Shivers falsely attributed to cold
Secrets revealed
Only by the moon's light
Moments of intimacy expressed
In gentle kisses
Flashes of burning passion
Frozen in memory by a cool wind
Questioning caresses answered
In the light of the moon shining on us
Walking in the moonlight
Never felt quite the same after you
How I long to share another
Midnight walk with you
Just one more will be enough, I lie to myself
Meet me there, you know where, under the moon
I'll show you all I hid then
I'll give you all I didn't have then
I'll open all I held locked inside then
Just tell me
Do you ever stare into
The moon's face
Remembering

Midnight walks we shared
The memories of almost moments
The moments our eyes told what our hearts couldn't say
The truth of us
Shared in midnight walks
Under the moon
Say you'll be there, under the moon
And, I promise, so will I

Shadow

You handed me a pretty pink flower
I held it gently, tenderly
Watched as your love turned to shadow
Knowing it was real and yet not
A mere shadow of what it once was
I held the pretty pink flower
Wondering we could find intimacy again
Finally feeling the ache of truth
Once a shadow, love's connection drifts away
And still I held that flower to connect me to you
Because letting go of the shadow of your love
Meant letting go of my last connection to you

Red Rose

You handed me a red rose
I felt only the thorn pricking my finger
A drop of blood fell on the perfect green stem
The beauty of the rose tainted
I watched the petals fade to rusty brown
Unwilling to release the rose from my grasp
The petals fell to the floor
One, then another, and another, then a bunch
Still I couldn't let the rose go
I watered it
I fed it
I nourished it
I tried every trick to prolong its life
Finally one day I awoke and stared at the rose
A thorny stalk bereft of its brilliant, velvety flower
My tears fell to the floor
Staining the dry, rusty brown petals
Turning them red again with dampness
Reminding me of the rose's former glory
I grasped the darkening green stalk in my hand
Taking pleasure in the thorns punching holes in my skin
Blood trailed down the green
Stripes mirroring the color of the once red petals
Drying to a rusty brown
My salty tears smearing the stripes
And then you were gone…

Autumn Regrets

Leaves of orange, yellow, brown
Cold wind blows
Through the recesses in my heart
You left behind
When you walked away
That Autumn day
When Autumn comes around
I always remember
How we started in Summer
And lasted until
That cold, rainy Autumn day
I saw you holding an umbrella over her head
My insecurities jumped to conclusions
Without giving you a chance to explain
I breathed in a cold, rainy breath of Autumn air
That settled into my heart
Forever to reside there
Leaving me with an emptiness I didn't understand
Forcing me to recognize that I wanted something more
Making me regret saying the words that tore us apart
Even today when Autumn begins
Our end haunts me
Making me wish
I could change the past as easily as
The leaves turn orange, yellow, brown
The warm wind turns icy
The sunny skies turn cloudy
Summer's brightness becomes Autumn's dullness
I wish I saw beauty in Autumn's multicolored leaves
But all I see is
Dying and decay

Loss and heartache
Regret
Autumn

Bluff

I won the bluff
Or rather
My bluff worked
You followed the rules
Of the game I created
The rules I changed at will
The rules designed to protect my heart
The rules that forced me to guard my hand
To hold the bluff
To force you to fold
Even though you held the better hand
Even though if you'd played your hand
We both could've won
Had we played as partners
I dreamed of you
Calling my bluff
Forcing me to show my cards
Making me reveal not only my hand but my heart
But you believed my bluff
You never knew my fantasy for us
Hidden beneath an exterior of independence and bravado
I hid it well
Beneath a poker face
That left me in tears
That broke my heart
That hurt you, too
That cost us the possibility of us
Before we could even truly start
So I stared at a hand that if revealed
May have actually brought us both a win
If I'd had the courage to play it

Instead I bluffed
Pretended I didn't care
Pretended we didn't have a chance
Pretended your cards held no potential for us
Pretended my cards offered no future for us
To play as partners
I bluffed my way right out of your life
When all I wanted was all you had to offer
Nothing more, nothing less
Sometimes I look into my heart
Review those cards
See they were better than I thought
And that's when I wish
You'd called my bluff
Demanded we play as partners
Instead you folded
And we lost the riches of us that could've been

Tipped Your Hand

You tipped your hand once again
You showed me a glimpse of truth
Now you're trying to put your poker face back on
Silence isn't the answer
It only makes me remember
The hand filled with hearts you displayed
In that unguarded moment
When you forgot to keep your cards hidden
I saw the hand you have to offer
Regardless of your bluff
Yet how can I argue
You're only doing what I did
So long ago
Running away every time
You tip your hand
I'm so familiar with the move
I think I may have taught it to you
Fear of losing if revealed
Always results in loss
Proving you were right even if you weren't
You tipped your hand once again
Now I wait for you to think I've forgotten
The hearts you displayed
Oh, how well I know that game
Oh, how much I hate that I played that bluff
Over and over and over again
But I know the rules
I taught them to you
So go ahead
Play my game just as I taught it
Just remember I can always change the rules

And then where will you be
Without me, perhaps…
Is that what you want?
My game cost me you
All those years ago
Honestly, I don't want to play anymore
Just show me your cards
I'll show you mine
Together we likely have the perfect hand

Medal

In your palm
You hold a medal
Earned for your service
I'm proud of you
I tell you so
What I don't say
What I can't say
My eyes pause on the medal
But stare at your fingers
Long, sexy, perfect fingers
I can't pull my gaze from your fingers
A memory stirs
My body reacts
I squirm in my seat
I remember your fingers
Searing you into my skin
With a touch so gentle yet urgent
With a desire so hot
Even ice couldn't cool it
A memory stirs
Of your fingers
Tracing me
Memorizing me
Sometimes I swear I still feel
The burn of your fingers
Arousing desire in me
The mere memory of your touch
Sets the path your fingers travelled ablaze
And I dream of ice
Those tantalizing fingers
Caressing my breasts

Tickling my belly
Pausing as you look into my eyes asking without words
Teasing me as I nod barely able to respond
Feeling the burn of your touch setting my cells on fire
I sigh and force my eyes back to
The medal in your palm
I give the nice response
Keep my naughty thoughts hidden
What I really want to say is
Oh, yes, you deserve a medal
And so do your fingers
I bite my lower lip
The thought occurs to me
If you held that medal in your lips
Oh, the memories that would conjure

Dream of Yesterday

There resides within my heart
The dream of yesterday
You populate that dream
A better me reaches for you there
We smile at one another
We laugh loudly and without hesitation
We embrace with unbridled passion
We love without reservation
The pain that is reality doesn't exist
We never spoke those words that destroyed us
We held one another through the bad moments
We strengthened one another during weakness
We never severed our connection
We never lost one another, not even for a moment
I see you now
The look in your eyes makes me wonder
If perhaps
A dream of yesterday
Also resides in your heart
If I populate that dream
If you also reach for me there
Will the day ever come when
We admit
The dream of yesterday
That resides in our hearts
Has the potential to become
The dream of tomorrow
If we make it
The reality of today
Until then
There resides within my heart

The dream of yesterday

Twenty Again

When you look at me
I feel twenty again
Sexy and tiny
Desirable and shy
Confident and flirty
Lost in new desire

When you speak to me
I feel twenty again
Dying to know more
My heart anticipating tomorrow
Scared you'll disappear
Lost in your words

When you listen to me
I feel twenty again
Heard and understood
Anxious to share me with you
My soul longing for connection
Lost in vulnerability

When you encourage me
I feel twenty again
Confident and strong
My dreams achievable
Life full of possibility
Lost in my head

When you smile at me
I feel twenty again
My body aches for your kiss

My lips tremble into a hesitant smile
My imagination conjures you next to me
Lost in the memory of passion's embrace

When you reach across the distance
I feel twenty again
Longing for your touch
Wanting you to love me
Scared you'll disappear when you know me
Lost in desire for what could be

Twenty

Twenty years ago
I faced a decision
To walk away
Or
Take a chance
To reveal my true feelings
Today
I face a similar one
Is this possible?
Is this real?
It's too close to the dream I had
Once I'd made my decision
Once I'd chosen my path
A part of me always knew
Someday I'd face this
Signs have appeared to remind me
To never let me forget
Reminders of little moments
Reminders of you
Reminders of what we were, or almost were
Reminders of the chance I never gave you
Mementos stored carefully among others
The tiny scar on my arm I grew to cherish
The places remotely related to you
Living on a street with your name
Hearing your voice on the street, or was it?
Seeing your twinkling eyes in a crowd, or were they?
Dreaming of you for no good reason
That pinch in my heart at each reminder
Pretending I'd forgotten you
Pretending you'd never been that important to me

Pretending you never crossed my mind
Pretending that pinch in my heart didn't mean anything
Pretending none of it mattered
Pretending always pretending
Convincing myself you hated me
Reminding myself you were better off without me
And then you were back
I felt those old emotions surfacing
I ignored them
I fought them
They became dreams
They became fantasies
I fought them harder
Finally, I acknowledged them
And realized
They were stronger than I'd ever admitted
Even to myself, maybe especially to myself
And then you moved on
Just when I worked up on the courage to tell you
Opportunity lost again
So I returned to my life
Such as it was
Tried to pretend again
Tried to make it work again
Tried to concentrate on your flaws
Tried to convince myself we wouldn't work anyway
Tried to blind myself again
But
It didn't matter
My heart refused the pretense
My memories of you surfaced and resurfaced
My emotions became complicated
I fought it
I needed simplicity

I compared you and him just like
Twenty years ago
I hid
I pretended
I went quiet
Then you were back again
Saying words I wanted to hear
Never quite saying exactly the right ones
But close, too close
We grew closer and then closer
Was it all in my head?
Friendship and attraction could no longer be denied
We pulled away again and again and again
Both of us retreated from the closeness we felt
Running back to the safety of the known
Avoiding the risk
Avoiding the vulnerability
Avoiding the pain we'll inflict
When the truth surfaces
When we can no longer fight it
When we finally realize
We are worth the risk
And yet I can't forget
Twenty years ago
I walked away
I chose the offer presented
I thought it was my choice
Now I realize
You had a choice, too
Yet you didn't make a move either
I know what I want now
But the choice has to be yours to make this time
If you knew the truth in my heart
Would you risk being vulnerable to me

Would you choose me
Would you even acknowledge what I see in your eyes
Then again
Maybe I'm only seeing what I want to see
Twenty years ago
You could've come after me
You could've demanded I reveal my heart
You could've coerced the truth hidden even from me
You could've called my bluff
You could've changed my choice
But you let me control everything, even our end
Was that fear?
Was it a sign of weakness?
Was it that you never loved me?
Is that what you're doing now?
Giving me control but not
Leaving me waiting but not
Toying with my heartstrings but not
Trying to let me lead when I don't want to
You're always there when I reach out
You reach toward me but hold back
But I need you
To make a move now – a real move beyond the superficial
To take a risk
To show me
You're willing to invest as much as I am
Until you do
I must wonder
Will it take another twenty years
For us to figure this out
To be honest with each other
To be vulnerable
To admit the truth
Will we both be

On our deathbeds with other loves
Pining for the one who got away
Regretting that we didn't take this chance
Wondering if we could've found true happiness together
We only get one life
I don't think I can handle another
Twenty years
Dreaming, thinking, fantasizing, wishing
Wondering what if
Twenty years ago
Twenty years from now
What about today
What about you
Do you want to wait another
Twenty years
Or
Perhaps forever works for you

Ask

All you ever had to do was ask
I waited for you to speak the words
But you never did
I listened for them between shared moments
I searched for them in your movements
I fantasized them in your absence
Maybe you said them and I never heard
I was prone to missing the message
Though I think I would've heard those words
I wanted you to say them so very much
I still do
You drop little hints
You almost say it
You pull away
Just like I did then
Sometimes I look into your eyes
And I see the question
I so wanted you to ask
Still wish you would ask
You remain silent even now
Sometimes I look at you
And I think
I created me
When I broke you
Still
Ask me today
I'll say yes

Sparks

Sparks of creativity
Jump through my brain
Giving form to scattered thoughts
Instigating new ideas
Flaming my thoughts with passion
Screaming at my muse
Burning my words with emotion
Grabbing my heart in memory's grip
Thoughts, emotion, passion
Always lead to memory
And memory always leads to you
So there are times I fight
Sparks of creativity
In hopes I won't think of you
Yet you never really leave my
Thoughts, emotions, passion
The memory of you is too strong
The memory of you is too significant
The memory of you is too pleasurable
The memory of you is too desirable
So I cling to
Sparks of creativity
Hoping to drink the elixir
Of memories of you
Hoping the poison of the present
Can be cured by
Sparks of creativity

Frozen Fire

Our fire burned bright
Ignited by ice
Freezing it in time
A lost ember frozen
Ready for rediscovery
Melting in our heat
As we struggle to preserve
Passion's fire
Trapped in frozen wonder
Beautiful testament to love's memory
We stare into the ice
Memorializing what was
Rather than grasping
What could be
Refusing to see
Love held frozen in time
Has no chance to grow
No matter how beautiful the memory

Ice

The heat of passion
Inflamed by ice
The ice of a broken heart
Thawed by love
A frozen moment in time
Heated by memory
Hot tears
Frozen into icicles
Love's possibility
Locked in an iceberg
Of lost heat
Your words melt
The block of ice
That trapped me
In a burning hell
All because I remember
When
Ice
Inflamed passion's heat

You Built a Fire

You built a fire
In the embers of my heart
I welcomed the kindling
You bestowed upon me
Flattery
Casual flirtatiousness
Compliments
After a time you added
A dry log upon the fire
Stoking the fire in my heart
Built by you
With the expression of your desire for me
With your appreciation of me
With the laughter you brought to my life
As the dry log burned quickly
I wondered what came next
I watched it burn to embers
Waiting on your next move
Hoping you wouldn't let our fire die
Even as the flames flickered
Slowly you added a green log
Testing before laying it gently
Upon the fire in my heart
Knowing that moving too quickly
Could douse the fire you'd built
As the flames licked the green log
With the passion you brought me
With the compassion you showed me
With the love for me you expressed
Day after day
You add kindling

You add dry logs
You add green logs
In just the right proportions
To keep my heart burning
With the fire you built

Ice Ignites Fire

Ice, ice, ice
Seems I can't get away from ice
Bringing a smile to my lips
Revealing my innermost yearnings
Yummy memories of melting ice slithering over my flaming skin
Aching to feel the thrilling cold against my scorching heat
Nerve endings ablaze with icy pleasure
Remembering makes me quiver every time
Unable to forget the time ice set me on fire
Ice, ice, ice
Titillating my fiery passion
Lighting fire to my frozen fantasies
Capturing the steam of my unquenchable desire
Reliving memories of nice's ice feeding naughty's flame
Ice, ice, ice
Jogging loose that memory again
Tempting me to embrace the ardor inflamed by ice
Ice, ice, ice
We never dreamed ice could ignite an inextinguishable fire

Embers of Us

I placed the embers of us
In a tiny box
Watched them burn out
Embers among fading ashes
Closed the lid
Locked it securely
Discarded the key
Tucked it away in
A hidden recess in my heart
Cherished though it was
I hid it even from myself
Little sparks ignited on occasion
Leaking into my heart's vulnerability
Lighting my passion
Reminding me we once loved
One day I finally felt strong enough
So I sat stark naked in the grass
Except for protective gloves
I removed the box from its hiding place
Broke the lock
Breathed in deeply
Flipped up the lid
Sparks of our love glowed
Drifted into the open
As I watched, waiting
The embers grew bolder, stronger, brighter
I stared into the embers flaming into a glow
Our love was always so bright
Containment was impossible
Now I wait for it to envelope me
Burning you into my soul once again

Or consuming me
Creating embers of me turning to ashes
Or giving me strength to step into myself
Lifting me higher than I've ever been
I'm no longer afraid of the love you offer
Now I only fear I waited too long
To free the embers of us
I trapped in a box

Key

You handed me a key
I froze it
I burned it
I fossilized it
I tossed it into the wind
It endured the torture I inflicted
It remained intact
It was, after all
A key imbued with love

Keyhole

I peek through the keyhole
Wanting to see all of you
Seeing only what you allow
It's my own fault
I threw away the key you gave me
When I walked away from you
Now I wish I'd hidden the key someplace safe
At least then it would be accessible, even if forgotten
I search for a way to unlock the door between us
I feel your resistance
To give me a new key
To let me in
So you show me
A glimpse of who you are now
Pulling me in
Feeding my fantasy
Making me want more
Holding back just enough
Protecting yourself from me
You fear if you let me in
I'll hurt you again
I promise I won't
But we both know you have good reason
To avoid giving me the key to see all of you
Our history isn't so easily forgotten
Even when viewed through its own keyhole
So
Until you're ready to give me a new key
To see all of you
I peek through the keyhole

Tightrope of Love

Tightrope of love
Barbs puncture vulnerability
Beauty and innocence
Left bloody and scarred
I see you on the other side
I step forward
Only a slight hesitance
I consider the rewards
I contemplate the barbs
Is the promise of us
Worth the risk of reopening old wounds
Is standing still
Worth forgoing the rewards of us
I look again
See your smile, your eyes beckoning me
Take my first step toward the future
Wonder if you'll meet me halfway
Traversing the barbs on the
Tightrope of love

Mirage

New love
Or perhaps old love rekindled
A mirage
Of beauty, light, and air
Amidst
The reality
Of grime, loneliness, and pollution
Encroaching
Ever-shrinking
Love's mirage
Blinds
Deafens
Traps
Against reality
Until
The two collide
Leaving the distinctly vague
Memory of
A mirage lost, unobtainable
The desire to recapture
The mirage
Amidst
Reality

I Feel You

I feel you
You invade my dreams
You've captured my heart
You've infiltrated my imagination
You've bombed the barricade surrounding me
You've imprisoned my willpower
I try to push you out
It makes no sense
Nothing can come of it
The time
The distance
The memories
The heartache
Our lives
None of it supports
You in my life
Or
Me in yours
Yet
Constantly, always
I feel you

Tear Forms

A tear forms
You're on my mind again
I remember a special moment shared
I forget a heartache inflicted
I long to tell you my true feelings
I long to reach out to you
I long to beg you to embrace the possibility of us
I long to beg you to embrace... me
I want you to love me
I want you to remember a special moment shared
I want you to forget a heartache inflicted
I want you to hold me again
I want you to kiss me again
I want you

A tear forms
My tongue won't form the words
The sound won't pass my lips
The action won't happen
I fear your response too much
So I imagine telling you
I run scenarios through my mind
I imagine your response
I imagine all the possible responses
I imagine you want me to love you
I imagine you want to remember our special moments
I imagine you want to forget the heartache we inflicted
I imagine you want me to hold you
I imagine you want me to kiss you
I imagine
You want me

A tear forms
Because I know in my heart
We belong together
We're good for one another
We bring out the best in each other
We offer exactly what the other needs
We have great potential
We've always had great potential
And yet we refuse to acknowledge that simple truth
Perhaps you fight the knowledge just as I do
Perhaps you fight the feeling just as I do
Perhaps you fight the connection between us just as I do
Or
Perhaps you never think about it
But I know a few minutes alone
Would answer the question of us
Instead of asking it

A tear forms
Instead of expressing the truth
Instead of expressing my thoughts
Instead of expressing my feelings
I do what I've always done when it comes to you
I fantasize
I run
I conceal
I hide
I never lie
I refuse to say it aloud
For fear you'll
Shrug
Run
Conceal

Hide
Lie
Say it aloud

A tear forms
As I imagine what we could be
If only we found the courage
To express what's in our hearts
To explore the possibility of us
Instead
A tear forms
Sometimes I blink it back
But
Sometimes I have no choice
Then it travels gently down my cheek
Or
Erupts into a full sob
Either way
When I think of
What we were
What we are
What we fight
How far apart we are
How connected we pretend we aren't
Those moments when the truth rises to the surface
Those moments we hint at exploring our real feelings
A tear forms…

Eyes

Don't be afraid
That's love you see in my eyes
Never judgment
Never cruelty
Only compassion
Only passion
You stop, your shadow quivers
You're sure you can't reach me
I've drifted away
The memory of me hovers larger than love
The trees fell stark in my absence
You stood staring across
The bridge of today that links yesterday to tomorrow
You turn your questioning gaze to my eyes
Knowing you never truly let me shine
For fear if I did
I'd burn us both to embers
Leaving passion's ashes to weep
As I float away
You still stand in the moment between past and future
That isn't quite present
Bare as a stark branch against a winter sky
A mere silhouette of possibility
You fear grasping
That's love you see in my eyes
Don't be afraid

Question

Your kiss a question
One I thought I'd answered
Yet there it is again
That hesitancy
That guarded passion
That wall around your heart
I recognize it
I owned it once
The wall I demolished
So I could love again
So I could live again
Or
Did I just give it to you
An unwelcome gift
To hold between us
To force distance
To create hesitancy
To keep
Your kiss a question

Guilt

I am not guilt-free
Nor am I guilty
We both played our parts
Deception of compromise
Words left unspoken
Moments left unlived
Searching for happiness
In moments that don't exist
Trying to force connections
That don't quite fit
Longing for the dream
We imagined, wanted, sought
Finding instead
Reality that doesn't fulfill
What should be but isn't
Love doesn't solve
Problems of incompatibility
When emotions rule one
And
Rationality rules another
Trying to be what you desired
Didn't fix us
Demanding you meet my image
Didn't fix us
When you are you
And
I am me
In all honesty
We aren't a we

Silence

Silence layers between us
As life progresses
We talk about everything
Everything except what matters
We nurture silence because
It keeps us from vulnerability
We have built walls
That allow us to stay together
Without truly connecting
We sit without words
Deceiving ourselves that is intimacy
A deception we need to not disintegrate
Silence keeps reality from interfering
With life's daily movements
Giving us reasons to ignore our pain
Ignoring yesterday's truth
In favor of today's fiction
As life pushes us toward tomorrow
We try to forget yesterday
Only to find the silence we cultivated
Dying in the soil we devotedly toiled
Deception and truth cannot grow together
Even when, especially when
Fertilized by silence

Questions

The words I wish to utter
I cannot say
There is no way to say them
At least not the right way
Their meaning is obscured by life
Their consequences revealed by love
No matter what the cost
I cannot utter them
I may lose you
I may lose everything
But I cannot utter
The words that most need spoken
If I reveal the truth
The entire truth
Too much will change too fast
We'll both be lost
In the chaos of uncertainty
Life's possibility may escape
As we try to find our footing
In the future of the unknown
As we remember yesterday
While embracing tomorrow
Where will we emerge
In the questions facing us today
Are the words I long to utter even true
Perhaps they are only
My imagination going wild
Perhaps they were only
What I wish could be true
Will I ever know the answers
To questions I cannot even voice

Trying

Today's meaning
Changes with tomorrow's influence
Watching you move ahead
Leaving you behind
How can both be true?
Yet they are
The connections not quite real
Yet not quite unreal
Confusion and chaos rule
The life we've created
Concealed in peace and quiet
Life moves forward
Lost in what could be
If not for what was
We are lost to one another
Yet we are forever connected
By moments shared
Where will we find truth
When deception is revealed
We live parallel lives
In the same house
Never seeing what matter to the other
Only missing what we need
Only wishing for what will fill the void
Left by our attempts to create a life
That can never be
We try so hard to be
What the other wants
Failing, always failing
Wishing by falling short
Wanting but not achieving

Pretending but not real
The life we've built
Can't find reality
No matter how hard we try

Crying in My Closet

I sat in my closet
Crying
Tears I didn't understand
Tears I can't explain
Tears I can't let anyone see
I felt the wet saltiness flow down my cheeks
I let them cascade without reservation
I embraced them for a moment
Tears I hold secret
For if I exposed them
They might reveal too much
I might not be able to hold back
I might lose the grip I have on my life
I might lose control of my emotions
I might lose me
Or worse yet
I might find me
In the wreckage of my mistakes
So
Day after day
Night after night
I sit in my closet
Crying

Blocked

The words are stuck
Hidden beneath anger
Smothered by pain
Choked by resentment
Living inside
Bleeding through silence
Imprisoned by fear
Dying for release
Struggling against despair
The words that define
The experience
The lesson
The reason
The changes in mind
The changes in spirit
The changes in heart
The words that have power
Healing or hurtful
Freeing or constricting
Loving or hateful
Accepting or excluding
The words are stuck
Just below the surface
Unspoken
The past, present, and future
Blocked

Music in My Heart

The music in my heart
You never understood
You only pointed out it was off-key
As it sailed past you
Into the night's shadows
You never paused
To recognize the love driving it
Only the mistakes
When my fingers slipped
And the tune failed
You never stopped
To recognize the passion spilling forth
As you pointed out my faltering notes
My rushed tempo
My missed cue
As I poured my love
Into the music in my heart
Giving you the best of me
Off-key, out of tune, screeching, off tempo
Though it may have sounded to you
Someone on the river
Under the moon
In the night's shadows
Will appreciate my efforts
Will understand I offered my best
Will recognize that
Though not perfect
I always played with love
I always played with passion
Thus finding the beauty in
The music in my heart

Ring

You slipped a ring
On my finger
I wanted it
I needed it
I didn't like it
You picked it out
I stood next to you and nodded
You loved it
You thought it was "me"
I looked at it
Thought it was you
Felt it encircle my finger
Felt it change my life
Felt it alter me
I went from strong and independent
To wife
I turned away from fun and laughter
To responsibility and seriousness
I left behind ambition and dreams
For companionship
I gave up me
For you
I chose to accept
The ring you chose
I threw that ring away
In a fit of anger
In a moment of wanting me
More than you
You picked out another ring
I didn't have the courage to say
That's not the one I want

I couldn't dash the joy on your face
You knew, just knew, you'd gotten it right
I stood beside you eyeing the one I really liked
But accepting the one that made your eyes shine
I didn't have the courage to say
That's not the one I want
Maybe what I really didn't have the courage to say
Was
I don't want
A ring, any ring
No ring will make me happy
A ring is simply a shiny circle of metal
Tying me to you
And
You to me
In the end
A ring is nothing
If the connection splits apart

Second Chances

We demolished our first chance
Or to be more accurate
I demolished our first chance
You stood by openmouthed
Gasping for air
Trying to save me from myself

We obliterated our second chance
Or to be more accurate
I obliterated our second chance
You stood by closemouthed
Letting me set all the rules
Watching me self-destruct

We annihilated our second second chance
Or to be more accurate
No, that is accurate
We kept our silence and pretended
Our feelings didn't exist
Our story was already finished in days long past

Now we have our second second second chance
Is there such a thing?
We grow close
We pull back
We speak quietly
We speak in code
We go about our lives, such as they are
Never quite being completely honest
Yet never quite lying
We help each other

We support one another
We try to pretend we're only friends
But
When we look into each other eyes
When we share that knowing smile
When we talk about everything, nothing
When we ignore what we both avoid
When we share a vulnerable moment
We both know
We're only going to get so many second chances
And neither of us wants to risk this being
Our final second chance
What if we destroy it again?
What if we find excellence with one another?
How many second chances can we waste?

Inevitable

Inevitable
We stand on the cusp of life
Looking at what we have
Thinking about what we lost
Wishing for a different reality
Longing for something better
Wondering if this is all there is
We lament possibilities abandoned
We regret today's pain
We consider future potential
And realize we've travelled many paths
Trying to make life the dream we desire
We stare into each other's eyes
Seeing what we cost one another
We listen to the silence that echoes
The desires we hid from one another
We touch each other's skin
Feel the emptiness of disconnection
We taste one another's despair
Over dreams denied in futile hope
We smell each other's disappointment
For a life built on illusion
We spoke words that ended the delusion
We'd lived for an eternity
We ripped off the blindfold
That allowed us to pretend we were perfect
We placed ourselves on the path toward
A future without one another
Then turned back wondering…
Eventually we will have to face the
Inevitable

For today we'll just continue to pretend
Perhaps tomorrow we'll also pretend
But someday soon
There will be no choice
We'll run out of way to hide
We'll no longer be able to run
We'll have to face the truth
We'll have to accept the
Inevitable

Gutted

I gutted myself
The truth spilled out
I didn't stop it
I took the knife
Plunged it into my vulnerability
Watched my fears bleed out
Stain everything around me
You watched me as I watched
The infection of secrets
Seep out onto the memories
You encouraged me
To reveal all of me
To risk bleeding to death
In order to cleanse old wounds
In order to finally heal
In order to let my journey
Help someone else
You smiled
Said the words I needed to hear
Didn't tell me to hide me
Didn't tell me to deny me
Didn't make me feel unclean
Didn't treat me as if I was infectious
Didn't act as if I was unworthy
You simply reminded me
Sharing what happened to me
Might help someone else
When the overwhelming fear hit
You didn't dwell on it
You didn't point it out
You gave me what I needed

A distraction
So I'd stop focusing on
The gaping wound
Bleeding my vulnerability
Onto every surface
I wonder
Will you be there when the wound heals?

You Broke Me

Some days
I forget
Some days
I can think of nothing else
All these years later
The moment
You broke me
Rings through my memory
At the most inopportune times
Interrupting my happiest moments
Stifling the laughter I want to release freely
Strangling the love I wish I could feel
Smothering the connection I long to experience
Stealing my strength
Erasing my confidence
Freezing me in a memory I wish never happened
I attempt to thaw myself by releasing the memory
I attempt to forget we ever met
I rewrite my confidence
I grab hold of my strength so tightly it struggles to breathe
I reach out to connect again and again and again
I offer love however flawed
I laugh even when the laughter chokes me
I welcome happiness whenever it's proffered
Yet every time I think the memory is gone
Every time I remember I survived
Every time I strive to thrive
Every time I embrace the whole of me
Every time I feel I am wonderful
The moment
You broke me

Rings through my memory

One Day a Year

I tried to forget
I tried to not remember
I tried to pretend
I tried and tried and tried
Yet the day approaches
As it does every year
My body reacts before my mind catches up
The day closing in on me
Breaking me down yet again
It's been so long
And yet I can't leave it behind
My heart aches with the memory
As I try once again to push it away, bury it
Try to kill it knowing it won't die
Oddly for the first time I wondered
If he remembers
If this date holds significance for him
I doubt it
He probably never bothers to remember
The day he destroyed the girl I was
The day he created his victim
He never understood the pain he inflicted
Not that it matters
Yet I can never forget
Victim one day a year
Survivor all the rest
Why can't I stop being his victim
He swore I'd never forget him
I guess he was right about that one
As much as I hate to admit it
As much as I want to prove him wrong

As my body closes into a ball
As my mind fights off the memory
As my soul struggles to remember me before...
As my heart longs to release the pain
I remember every detail
I remember every nuance
I remember every tear
I remember...
Tears threaten the corners of my eyes
And I try once again
To forget
To not remember
To pretend
I attempt to shut out
His face, his voice, his touch
Only to fail as the memory invades my body once again
It is written on every cell
It is painted on every tear
It is there
It taints everything good in my life
Even today, all these years later
The day approaches
I lose myself all over again
But I'll wake up when the day is over
And
I will love myself again
I will still be here
I am a survivor
I am strong
I may never forget
But
I decide who I am
I control my life
I move forward

I survive
I thrive
I won't let him
Ruin more than one day a year
Even if I have to give up that one day a year
For the rest of my life
In order to survive all the other days
In order to thrive all the other days
One day a year
Is the cost I don't deserve to pay
For an act I didn't commit
Yet no matter what
I'm always charged that
One day a year

Anger Rages

Anger rages through my memories
Memories of betrayal and heartbreak
Anger, though, simply masks the emotions
Driving me into silence
Anger bubbles up to the surface
Infecting my heart and soul
Splitting my skin apart
Cracking my bones
Inflaming my organs
When memories invade my happiness
Anger seeps around the edges
Spilling into my life
Leaving me longing for the memories
That lift me out of anger into joy
Sometimes even happy memories
Spark a thread of anger
Reminding me of
What was
What could've been
What isn't
All because of the decisions I made
When memories didn't seem important
Living felt more important than memories
Yet every life moment is a memory in process
Memories raging with anger or glory
Are memories nonetheless

Girl

I tried to be a good girl
I boxed up my naughty impulses
Stored them in the recesses of my mind and heart
Tried to pretend I hated the unruly part of me
Searched for a way to be happy
Concealing my fantasies under a sweet smile
Imprisoning my risqué desires inside ambition's drive
Knowing if I unleashed all of me you would leave
One day I exploded, or rather imploded, from the pain
All of my needs, desires, sensuality refused to be contained
The bad girl in me banged her fists against my chest and screamed
I'd denied her much too long
She wanted to be liberated
She held all the secrets to my joy in life
The good girl in me even denied herself happiness
Why couldn't she be content with what was given her
Why did she listen to the bad girl
Whispering those possibilities
Showing those fantasies
Driving her toward pleasure
I like the bad girl in me
She lives for herself without apology
The good girl in me lives for everyone else
And is always apologizing for not being enough
I tried to be a good girl
But the bad girl in me is so much more enjoyable…

Mama Doesn't Need to Know

Mama doesn't need to know
How much I enjoyed the cheap bourbon
Glass after glass after glass
Or that I danced until the bar closed
Laughing until my throat hurt
Or that I enjoyed grinding against that handsome stranger
Feeling the rise my touch gave him
Or that I handed him the wrong phone number with a giggle
Wondering if he would notice it spelled FOFF
Or that I kissed him passionately before I walked away
Giving him something to remember
Or that I called the man I truly desired, perhaps even loved
And pretended I only wanted sex just to have his attention
Or that I spent the night in his arms
And it was glorious
No, no, no
I'm thinking
Mama doesn't need to know
Her good girl is actually quite naughty at heart
So please don't tell her
Because really, truly
Mama doesn't need to know

Boxed Secrets

Inside our minds
Inside our hearts
Inside our bodies
We wrap up little boxes
We tie little bows around the boxes
We store the boxes safely
The little boxes conceal the secrets
We hide from the world
We hide from those we love
We hide from those who love us
We hide from ourselves
Those boxes stack on top of one another
Wedge into the empty spaces
Get smashed against one another
Banged, crushed, cracked
The concealed secrets leak
Into our memories
Into life's moments
Into our actions
The boxes topple over
The secrets get knocked around
Jostled, bruised, battered
Pushing against who we are
Pulling on who we want to be
Pressing down who we were
Boxes concealing secrets
Create the people we are
Hide the truth of us
Allow us to survive
Boxes concealing secrets
Implode

Our true selves escape
Our inner strength shines
Our flaws are revealed
Boxes of secrets
Hold us hostage
Set us free
Always struggle to remain
Boxes filled with secrets
Ready to give the world
The present concealed within
The truth of who we are
Hidden in
Boxes of secrets

Promise of Spring

Cloudy skies turn bright blue
And back to cloudy gray
The sun teases and tempts
Retreats after tricking
Bare branches bud
Blooms burst from buds
A warm day tantalizes
A cold day reminds
Back and forth
The days vacillate
Like a fickle lover
Teasing, tempting, titillating
Making promises
Hiding behind yesterday
Trying to emerge anew
Showing renewal
Expressing growth
Dragging us along
On a journey
As green becomes greener
Tulips open their colorful lips
Daffodils burst forth
The grounds thaws
Like the heart
Of a new lover
Allowing growth
To show tender shoots
Easily destroyed under
Careless feet
Tentatively accepting
Warmth, support, love

Searching for renewal
Emerging anew
As is the
Promise of Spring

Talk Kentucky to Me

Talk Kentucky to me
I shake my head at your request
I smile a shy smile
We both know the shyness is false
The words already reverberate in my skull
Like the ball in a pinball machine
I apply a slight drawl to my reply
"But I don't wanna"

Talk Kentucky to me
Images crash through my mind
Staring at the television as a small girl
Watching Walter Cronkite speak
Mimicking his facial movements
Holding my lips like his
Matching my tone to his
Finding his rhythm

Talk Kentucky to me
Words pronounced as other words
Should I say radish or reddish
For that pink skinned root vegetable
Should I say hollow or holler
For that valley where we live
Should I say creek or crick
For the stream of water flowing in front of the house
Should I say picture or pitcher
For the artwork on the wall

Talk Kentucky to me
Charm me with colloquialisms

Might as well take the night
He's dumber than a box of rocks
She sure does get around
He'll never amount to a hill of beans
Well, you know he ain't had much raisin'
Bless your heart
        Lessens any harsh comment

Talk Kentucky to me
I worked so hard
To speak without an accent
To sound intelligent
To leave behind the "dumb hick" label
To train my tongue to wrap around the words
To learn proper pronunciation
To find my own voice

Talk Kentucky to me
I give in with a sweet smile
Embracing my heritage
Appreciating my roots
Loving my home state
Missing the slow drawl and lazy words
Feeling my place in the world

Talk Kentucky to me
I finally drawl
Whatta you want me ta say?
Wanna take the night with me?
You shore ain't dumb as a box a rocks
Bless your heart, hon
'Cause you know, that's nice
With a wink and just the right inflection

Now, talk Arabic to me
You smile slowly and shake your head
Mock my Kentucky accent
"But I don't wanna"
I smile, give my best puppy dog eyes, and whisper, please
You give in whispering in my ear
Shukran, Habibiti
Bahebik
I return
You're welcome, honey
I love you, too

Memory of Kentucky Summers

The lush green hills of Kentucky
Humidity-laced, tobacco- scented air
Sunshine casting a blue tint on grass
Fields of corn waltzing in the air
Horses grazing lazily
Tails swatting flies from their backs
Cattle wading belly deep in a cool pond
Long, hot days in the fields
Trying to look attractive in shorts and bikini tops
Sweat trickling between breasts
Picking green beans, tomatoes, and blackberries
Hoeing fields of tobacco
Preserving garden food for winter
Swimming in the local creek
Exploring the woods around the house
Softball at the old vacant red brick school
Drive-in movies with friends
Passing notes about boys during church
Sundays playing cards at Grandma and Grandpa's house
Friends and family wandering in and out of the game
Talk of crops, rain, and gardens
Catching up on the latest news and gossip
Laughter amidst hard work
Kentucky summers growing up
At heart I'll always be a Kentucky girl

Summer

Heat
      Sunshine
      Cool water
Brightness
      Blue skies
      Flowers
Green
      Grass
      Trees
Shade
      Outdoor
      Cool breeze
Tan
      Bikini
      Beach
Summer
      Swimming
      Fun

Kentucky

Kentucky remains my home in my heart
Kentucky is my birthplace
Kentucky showed me love
Kentucky holds my deepest heartache
Kentucky reminds me of my happiest moments
Kentucky won't let me forget my saddest times
Kentucky beckons me with The Derby, basketball, bluegrass
Kentucky welcomes me with family, friends, roots
Kentucky comforts me with memories of laughter, celebration, happiness
Kentucky warms me with sun, bourbon, passion
Kentucky smiles upon me the way only one who knows my core can
Kentucky goes with me no matter where I go
Kentucky is in my heart, soul, and body
Kentucky, how I tried to escape you
Kentucky, how I tried to forget you
Kentucky, how I tried to run from you
Kentucky, how I didn't understand you
Kentucky, you are me and I am you
Kentucky, I realize I can never escape you, never really wanted to
Kentucky, I love all you represent now that I quit blaming you
Kentucky, you'll always be home no matter where I live
Kentucky, you are my heart's home

Roots

Grounding me
Stretching to let me grow
Spreading as far as you are
Holding us together no matter the distance
Letting me branch out on my own
Nurturing me
Feeding me
Giving me a foundation
Providing a past
Allowing a future

Reaching Out

Reaching out
Across time
Across space
To say
You are remembered
You are important
You were never forgotten

Reaching out
Across time
Across space
To say
I miss you
I love you
I treasure you

Reaching out
Across time
Across space
To say
Let's talk
Let's laugh
Let's share life

Reaching out
Across time
Across space
To say
Family is forever
Friendship is cherished
Relationships mold us

Reaching out
Across time
Across space
To remind us all
We matter to someone

Logs

Standing on tiptoe on Daddy's red log truck
Reaching up, wanting to touch the top
The log too tall, its circumference enormous
To a ten year old girl
My tiny hand
Rubbed the cut on the end, smooth bits and rough spots
Pulled my hand away and stared at the sawdust
Wiped it on my shorts
Hoped Mom wouldn't notice
The scent of freshly cut timber
Permeated the air around me
Comforted me
Held me in its grasp
Others saw
A truck filled with large trees
Perhaps even judged my Daddy
Without knowing
His love for the woods
His care to preserve, conserve, sustain
His dedication to only take as much as needed
His determination to do no harm
I saw
The food those logs would put on the table
The house they paid for
The clothes they provided to cover me
The vacation my family would share
My Daddy's hard work
My Daddy's calloused hands
My Daddy's pride
My Mom's fear every time he went to the woods
My Mom's relief every time she heard the truck coming home

My Mom's agitation every time he was late, the woods were dangerous
Pride filled me, too
Daddy's love
Chained to a truck
In a stack of timber
Held in place by heavy, unyielding chains
Headed to a sawmill
For their next journey
To become
Someone else's home
Someone else's furniture
Someone else's dreams
That load of logs
Represented so much more
Than the trees they had been

Wisdom and Love

Last night I dreamed of
Grandma
Grandpa
Great Aunt Dot
Grandma's house
Filled with love and laughter
My three cats happy there
Laughter tasting sweet and unfamiliar on my lips
Grandma's hug
Grandpa's knee
Great Aunt Dot's laugh
I awoke from laughter and chatter
With tears on my face
And suddenly
I thought of you
You who shouldn't enter my thoughts
But always do
When I think of family
When I think of love
You who invades my dreams far too often
I reached out for Grandma, Grandpa, Great Aunt Dot
I reached out for wisdom
And ended up finding love
For perhaps
Love is wisdom
Wisdom is love
And then there were thoughts of you…

Grandma

I think of you with love
And I smile
When I cook I remember
Your table filled with everyone's favorites
Quiet afternoons remind me of
Your home filled with unexpected guests
Immediately welcomed
I recall with fondness
Sunday afternoons at your house filled with
Family, friends, neighbors
Playing cards, eating, laughing
Your never idle hands
Inspired me to try new things
The way you listen without judging
The encouragement and kinds words you give so freely
Showed me how to care
Even today
When I wrap myself in the quilt
You made me
It feels like you're hugging me
And my heart fills with appreciation
That I have a grandma like you!

Granny

Memories of you
Have begun to fade ever so slightly
I fear they'll desert me entirely one day
So I remind myself
Birthday cards with a few dollars, more than you could afford
Letters in college that encouraged and reminded
Always began
"My Dearest Granddaughter"
I thought it old-fashioned then
Now I cherish those words
I read every single letter with joy, hidden but real
Perhaps my love of books came from you
You read voraciously
Stacks of books and magazines cluttered your house
You read your chapters in the Bible each night
How many "most chapters read" pins did you win?
Family meant everything to you
Yet you lived alone much of the time
Widowed before I was born
Raised two of your grandchildren
You set an example of independence
Though I wouldn't recognize it for years
I reveled in your pride in my accomplishments
Drawers filled with mementos of your family's successes
Cherished quietly, privately, and yet not so privately
You bore responsibility for your life
Made things work when they seemed desperate
You were stronger than it appeared
I see that now
Perhaps I should've appreciated you more then
As I do now

Grandpa

Grandpa
Hope you know how often
You're remembered with love
Every time I put pen to paper
I'm grateful to you for encouraging
My "Groundhog" stories
When I meet someone new
I remember how everyone
Was always welcome in your home
I'll never forget your smile
When you said
"How's Pappaw's good girl?"
I'll always remember you singing
The song about Sally Goodin
That made me giggle
Listening to your stories of times past
Always left me with the feeling
Of connection to my history
Playing cards
Around your kitchen table
Created many cherished memories
I've always known you were proud of me
And I've always been proud
You were my
Grandpa

Lessons in Memories of War

I sat across the table, pen poised
Anxious to listen to your story
You slurped your coffee from a small plate
As was your habit
Lit a Lucky Strike
Inhaled deeply
Exhaled smoke away from me
Smiled at me
A mixture of emotions filled your features
I'd asked, innocently, for you to tell me of war
I expected stories of glory
I expected stories of heroism
I expected stories akin to history class
Instead you spoke slowly, reluctantly even
Pain filled your voice
The facts, the details
You delivered matter-of-fact, monotone at times
You told of K-rations, C-rations, hunger
Without dressing up the truth to make it palatable
You told of hopping on cargo planes for a momentary escape
With a gleam in your eye
You told of the destruction you witnessed
With regret on your face
You told of injuries and loss of life
Dare I ask, was that a tear you blinked back?
My strong Grandpa, was it a tear?
You told of driving General Patton
With pride in your voice
But nothing topped your conviction
That you did the right thing, the moral thing
When you defied orders

To save a German infant
My simple assignment
To hear about World War II from
Someone who'd been there
Lost its simplicity
As you spoke
You taught me
Real people fight and die
Real people take a stand
Real people make costly mistakes
Real people pay the price
Your memories illustrated
Like no history book can
War isn't glorious regardless of victor
War is dirty and difficult
War is painful and scary
War widows
War injures
War kills
War destroys innocence
War changes people and nations
War wounds even the unwounded

Let Us Remember

Let us remember
To hold each other tight
To love without hesitation
To give our hearts freely
To lift one another high

Let us remember
Those who came before
Those who touch our lives
Those who stood against injustice
Those who loved enough to make changes

Let us remember
The mistakes we've made
The lessons we've learned
The distance we've traveled
The changes we've accomplished

Let us remember
Diversity makes us strong
Unity breeds acceptance
Love conquers hate
Dreams for a better life unite us all

Let us remember
Today's action creates tomorrow's reaction
Today's conviction becomes tomorrow's action
Today's perception leads to tomorrow's conviction
Today's experiences leads to tomorrow's perception

Let us remember

We choose love
We choose hate
We choose peace
We choose war

Let us remember
Courage is loving when it hurts
Integrity is holding to principle when it's difficult
Freedom is most important when threatened
Fear threatens courage, love, integrity, principle, and freedom

Let us remember
Compassion destroys hatred
Acceptance erases intolerance
Education eradicates ignorance
Peace obsoletes war

Let us remember
To reach out with love
To open our hearts to compassion
To embrace our differences
To welcome peace when vengeance feels better

Let us remember
We decide with each thought
We choose with each action
We determine with each reaction
We choose every day

Let us remember
The importance of each thought
The importance of each action
The importance of each reaction
The importance of each day's choice

Let us remember
To listen to every point of view
To see the obvious and the not so apparent
To weigh each option
To choose wisely

Let us remember…

Why Do We Wait

Why do we wait
To say I love you
To wish for peace
To express gratitude
To slow down long enough to listen
To laugh
To play

Why do we wait
To be good to one another
To take time for each other
To celebrate family and friends
To check on family
To contact old friends
To reach out to loved ones, near and far

Why do we wait
To give freely of ourselves
To care if the poor are hungry or cold
To reach out to strangers
To wish one another happiness
To share good will
To bestow merriment

Why do we wait
When we could
Love, laugh, care, celebrate
Today
Everyday

Traditions

Past traditions respected
Family gathers together
Sharing joyous moments
Reminiscing
Children playing
Men discussing politics, crops, work
Women cooking, conversing, and laughing
Table full of favorites

New traditions created
Friends filling the family void
Laughter and conversation abound
Cooking a feast together
Fondly remembering family holidays
Toasting the future full of promise

Past traditions meet new
In hearts filled with joy, love, and gratitude
For friends that become family
And family that become friends
Creating everlasting bonds
With loved ones near and far

Holiday Memories

A house filled with loved ones
Laughter permeates the air
Stories shared one more time
Catching up on the day to day
Smiles touch faces
Someone far away fondly remembered
A serious moment
A beloved departed soul evoked
An unbreakable connection
From a past shared
From a future anticipated
Love flows from heart to heart
A simple glance expresses a welcome familiarity
Comforted by the knowledge
Acceptance and love can always be found
In the hearts of family and true friends

Lifelong Friendship

Lifelong friendship
Is the friendship
We most cherish

It's the friendship
We reach for when
When our lives fall apart

It's the friendship
Where we know
Our success will always be celebrated

It's the friendship
Where we never have to explain
Because our secrets are known

It's the friendship
That can pick back up
After years of silence and distance

It's the friendship
We turn to
When family fails us

It's the friendship
Whose memories comfort us
When we're sad

It's the friendship
Whose memories make us smile
When we're happy

It's the friendship
Built on the trivial and monumental
Moments of our lives

It's the friendship
That sets the bar
For all other friendships
Throughout our lives

Friendship

You and I
Twins in our hearts
Friendship that makes us sisters
Bonded by understanding that needs no words
When my heart aches
You reach out
Fingers and palms to mine
Knees to my knees
Head to my head
Heart to my heart
Sharing your energy
Reminding me I'm never completely alone
No matter how isolated I feel
Boosting my mood when it dips to dangerous levels
Relieving my pain when it threatens to destroy me
Encouraging my dreams when I feel like a failure
Offering me unconditional support when my optimism fails
Helping me see my truth when I'd rather hide from it
Coaxing my smile when tears stream down my cheeks
Giving me reason to laugh loudly when I take me too seriously
Giggling with me over the absurdity of life
Femininity enveloping our strength
No compromise of our beauty or resilience
As your energy infuses mine
I take what I need and store the rest aside
Ready to return the love when you need me
Two little girls, two grown women
Friendship through the years
Love that makes
Two strangers become friends
Two friends become sisters

Two sisters become angels
To one another

Connections

We vow
We'll never forget
We'll always be connected
We'll love endlessly
We'll cherish without hesitation
We'll hold memories close

Time passes
The memory tricks
The letters dwindle
The phone calls slowly disappear
Happy times fade
Wrongs seem less painful

A chance encounter
Brings new vows
To write more often
To call and chat more regularly
To remember what we once were
To move forward together

Life happens
We struggle
To share
Happy times and laughter
To hide
Painful moments and memories to keep peace
The little moments that make each day real
The little bits of our selves that connect us

We strive

To be more connected
To yesterday, today, tomorrow
To cherish
Old friends and new
To always remember to love

Reaching out
Knowing family, friends, acquaintances
Are still there
Appreciating each moment we share
Regretting the lost moments
Feeling the experiences that bind us to one another

Cross My Mind

Sometimes you cross my mind
Just a fleeting thought
Just a smile for no reason
A quickening of my heart
A song
A word
A picture
Just a moment in time
Your voice on the wind
Your smile on a stranger
Your walk in a crowd
A laugh across the room
A touch on my arm when no one's near
A kiss on the forehead waking me in an empty room
A sudden whiff of your cologne when I'm all alone
A happy moment I'd like to share
A sad moment suddenly comforted
Sometimes you cross my mind....

Barely

I heard a voice
Barely a whisper
My name on the wind
It sounded like you
I felt a hand
Barely a graze
Against my cheek
It felt like you
I saw a mirage
Barely a form
In the clouds
It looked like you
I responded
Barely a whisper
With your name
Carried away on the wind
I reached for your hand
Barely a grasp
The memory of your touch
Absorbed against my cheek
I looked into the mirage
Barely a form
As it drifted away into the sun
I reached for you
Only to remember
You left me behind
With only memories
Barely enough to hold
In my heart
Barely...

Presence

Today
I felt your presence
I was doing nothing special
Just going about my life
Typing words
Reading a book
Washing dishes
Folding clothes
Stirring a pot of sauce
Yet each motion
Each sensation
Brought to mind
A moment spent with you
In that memory
I heard your voice
Praising me
As if you stood next to me
I felt your hand
Guiding mine
As if you held it
I smelled your coziness
Enveloping me
As if you embraced me
I saw your smile
Welcoming me
As if I'd just entered your orbit
I tasted your kiss
Bringing me home
As if you'd just fed my soul
Today
I felt your presence

I was doing nothing special
Just going about my life
When your love touched my heart
Though you're no longer with me

Running

He stands on the hill
Their hill
Her hill
His hill
Looking at the stars
Their stars
Her stars
His stars
He thinks of her last words
"You have to understand"
As tears streamed down her face
His tears start
As he remembers his reply
"How can I? Why should I?"
He remembers her running
Running from him
Running from the past
Running from the present
Running from herself
Suddenly she stopped running
He remembers her disappearing
He realizes she's never coming back
He looks down at the ground
Feeling tears on his face
He begins to run
From the past with her
From the present without her
From the future without her
From himself all alone
He's trying to run to her
But he can never reach her

Even with his love
Because she's gone forever
Running….

Stolen

The world's tears fall
A nation mourns
A class's heart breaks
Once again
Opportunities snatched
Along with young lives
The People's Princess
A Nation's Son
An unknown sixteen year old
A late night car crashes
An evening flight lands on the ocean floor
A dirt bike smacks a tractor tire
Three lives snuffed out too soon
Three faces frozen forever in time
Speculations abound
The People's Princess could have changed lives
Her contributions endless
A Nation's Son could have been President
His charitableness boundless
The sixteen-year-old could have been anything
In his classmates eyes
His potential untapped and enormous
The People's Princess
Made real by her faults and pain
Loved for her elegance and style
A Nation's Son
Loved for his ordinariness
Admired for his grace and dignity
The unknown sixteen year old
Forever the beloved basketball player who might have...
Loved for his smile, sense of humor and generous heart

All forever young
Forever beautiful
Forever larger than life
Forever potential lost
The world
A nation
A class
Left to wonder
What did we lose
What opportunities were missed
What could have been
If only these young lives hadn't been
Stolen

Grief

My tears fall
I weep
Not for you
You were ready to go
But for what I've lost
Would I have ever been ready to let go?
Your presence in my life
Your voice saying
"I love you. I miss you."
Your eyes lighting up
When I enter the room
Your smile
When I tell you my dreams
Your hug
When I arrive and then leave your house
Your welcoming spirit
That embraced all
Your pride in me
For all that I achieved
Your support
When I chose a different path

My tears fall
I weep
But I'm grateful
I have memories
Of how you touched my life
Of all you taught me
Of laughter in your home
Of conversations - the serious and the absurd
Of a table full of favorites – food and people

Of every time your face lit up
Of every time I felt your love
Of your comforting embrace

Mostly I'm grateful
You were my grandparents

Paint My Grief

I paint my grief
Into your wings
As you leave your cage
So I may release it
So you may carry it away
The cage is closed
So it can't return
Still it is immortalized
In the strokes of sadness
In the lines of tears
In the paint's blackness
I paint my grief
Into your wings
To forever display
Its attempt at escape
Its desire to leave
Its need for release
I paint my grief
Into your wings
So I may remember
As I learn to laugh again

Winter

The wind is chilling
The fire cozy and warming
The sky dark and gloomy
The house bright and roomy

Diamonds sparkling across the snow
Inside a warm glow
A sheet of white across the field
Rooms all laughter filled

Bitter cold
Stories from the old
The night dreary
Family creating a new, happy memory

Fresh snow falling
Folks come calling
Snowmen in the yards
People playing cards

The trees are stark and bare
Home filled with care
Winter is here
Only room for cheer

Time Moves On

Precious moments lost
Minutes tick by
Hours accumulate
Days keep coming
Weeks don't slow down
Years absorb us
Moving forward
Standing still
Pain
Pleasure
Hate
Love
Experience continues
Good
Bad
Indifferent
The moment to savor
The pain that never ends
Lasting the same ticking minutes
Life only stops with death
Time moves on

Life in a Day

Life in a day
A single moment lived
Gone forever
Begins and ends
Waits for no one
Each moment starts
In the instance it ends
Every day begins
A new life
Each series of moments
Touch on one another
Build on one another
Each lost before it's recognized
A million lives
Lived in one
As each day
Begins and ends
Always resulting in
A life in a day

Leave

Today I shall
Leave
Behind yesterday
Moments that cut my heart out
Shall lose their power to bleed fresh pain
As I embrace lessons
The words we uttered
Cannot be erased
Carved in the stony regions of my heart
For all eternity
To remind us of their power
To change life's path
Today I shall
Leave
Behind yesterday
The hope of forgetting
The desire to change the unchangeable
The need to undo what already happened
The need to unsay the spoken words
The need to unthink the undesirable thoughts
The impossible
Today I shall
Embrace
What's left
What shall come
After
The way we acted
Yesterday

Life Story

Throughout life
We meet people
Who make an indelible impact
For better or worse
Sometimes they stay
Sometimes they go
Sometimes they return
But the imprint left on our hearts
Changes us forever
As we grow into the people we're meant to be
We grow to appreciate
All those who've played a role
In the creation of
Our
Life stories

Reality Creeps In

Reality creeps in
Grabs my imagination
Squashes creativity
Jams my life into a little hole
Breaks my will
Reminds me what I lost
Tortures me with memories
Leaves me with nothing
Comes with a vengeance
Wakes me up
Destroys all that is good
This is the life I've built
So I'll just fantasize
About the life I want
Until I can have it

Residue

Our lives collect residue
We can't help it
Though we may try
We move from place to place
Taking along beloved possessions
Leaving behind once-loved belongings
We walk away from relationships
Taking along memories of affection
Leaving behind traces of adoration
We release people from our orbit
Taking along little changes they caused
Leaving behind our influence on them
We walk this journey through life
Loving, touching, ignoring, accepting, rejecting
Never realizing the residue we collect
Never acknowledging the residue we leave behind
Residue that changes us and them
Residue that influences all future behavior
Residue that taints memories for better or worse
Though we may try not to
We can't help it
Our lives collect residue

Memories in Silhouette

Without knowing it
We move through life
Creating memories
Memories we'll cherish someday
A special love
A unique friendship
A cherished moment
An event that changes us forever
Without knowing it
We move through life
Creating memories
We wish we could forget
A broken heart, ours or someone else's
A friendship betrayed
A despised moment
An event that breaks our spirit
Without knowing it
We move through life
Creating memories
Creating the who of who we are
Finding our path to acceptance
Walking our journey to our best selves
Influencing others' lives
Creating memories
Memory that may seem
A silhouette of our lives
A life that becomes a
Memory in Silhouette

PRAISE FOR T. L. COOPER'S BOOKS

Reflections in Silhouette:

"...Brave enough to lower the curtain into her own heart, T.L. gives the reader that certain leverage where one might be able to find the strength, upon reflection, to go forward into the bright sunshine of their own new day..." - Ray Ellis, author of the Nate Richards Series.

Love in Silhouette:

"...Love in Silhouette" is a delightfully honest and open-faced collection of poetry that leaves you feeling as though you have peeked in on intimate moments of the author's love life..." - Mary Braun, co-author of Opposites Attract: A Haiku Tete-a-Tete.

"...T.L. Cooper's in-depth look at all aspects of this thing called love is so raw, honest, and truthful that at times the reader feels almost voyeuristic gazing in at the emotions that Cooper depicts so well..." - Stacey Rourke, author of The Gryphon Series.

"...As she travels the avenues and boulevards of the human condition, she explores the sensations of touch, sight, and the aromas of love's jubilations and the darkening grays of a broken heart... - Ray Ellis, author of the Nate Richards Series.

"...Cooper's poems are lyrical. Don't be fooled into thinking that this is simply a collection of silly love poems. They pull you in to explore the depths of love and all that goes with it..." - Lauren Carr, author of the Mac Faraday Series.

All She Ever Wanted:

"...A thoughtful, insightful look into the changing human mind and spirit evoked by an interracial friendship, All She Ever Wanted is a superbly written, highly recommended novel showcasing a theme that is as historic and universal as interracial human experience, and contemporary as today's newspaper headlines..." - Midwest Book Review.

ABOUT THE AUTHOR

T. L. Cooper grew up on a farm in Tollesboro, Kentucky. She earned a Bachelor of Science from Eastern Kentucky University. Her poems, short stories, articles, and essays have appeared online, in books, and in magazines. She published a novel, *All She Ever Wanted.* Her latest works are two books of poetry, *Love in Silhouette: Poems* and *Reflections in Silhouette: Poems.* When not writing, she enjoys yoga, golf, and traveling. To learn more, visit www.tlcooper.com.

www.ingramcontent.com/pod-product-compliance
Lightning Source LLC
Chambersburg PA
CBHW051832040426
42447CB00006B/484